HOW TO START OVER AFTER LOSING EVERYTHING

Sabat Beatto

Disclaimer

This book has been written for information purposes only. Every effort has been made to make this book as true, complete and accurate as possible. However, there may be mistakes in typography or content. Also, this book provides information relevant to starting over after losing everything as a result of a house fire. This information chronicles events up to the publishing date. Therefore, this book should be used simply as a guide.

The information provided here is not meant to be a substitute for professional legal or medical advice. These tips are from first responders, lawyers, insurance agents and people who have shared real-life experiences. Always check with a doctor, lawyer or appropriate professional before making any legal or healthcare-related decisions.

The purpose of this book is to educate and encourage. The author and the publisher do not warrant that the information contained in this book is fully complete and shall not be responsible for any errors or omissions. The author and publisher shall have neither liability nor responsibility to any person or entity with respect to any loss or damage caused, or alleged to be caused, directly or indirectly by this book.

Copyright

TABLE OF CONTENTS

DEDICATION

This book is dedicated to all those who have refused to give up but have instead chosen to start over even after experiencing a house fire that cost them everything.

These courageous people have inspired me to write this book as a helpful tool for them and the other millions who have suffered similar circumstances. Happy reading.

LETTER OF GRATITUDE TO MY FRIENDS OF P.S. 280Q

I called you a friend because we shared lunch together. I called you a friend because we passed each other in the hallway each day with a hello. I called you a friend because you asked about my family and how things were going with my life. You were just someone I passed by and called a friend because it seemed like the most polite thing to do.

Now, I call you a friend because you helped me out when I needed someone. You went out of your way to make sure my family and I were okay. You were there for us with prayer. How greatly you helped us through one of our darkest times. That is how I know you are a true friend. I may not be able to ever give back what you've given me. I cannot even begin to express the gratitude I have towards you. Thank you doesn't seem enough, but I know for sure that when you need me, I will be there for you just as you were for me. I thank you for being the kind-hearted person you are, for going out of your way when I had nothing and giving me something. Thank you for giving me hope. Thank you for all the prayers you prayed for my family. Thank you for taking your time to talk to me and encouraging me. Thank you for being a person I can count on and call a friend. I will never forget these actions which I will forever hold dearly!

Sabat Beatto

INTRODUCTION

It was a well-furnished and beautiful apartment graced with fanciful wallpaper. The sitting room was tastefully equipped with a flat-screen TV and a, just purchased, sound system. This abode was a theatre of beautiful memories. It was always fun-filled on Saturday nights and Sundays. We enjoyed Karaoke and also welcomed friends who came to read my latest writing. Alas, tragedy struck! The beautiful times were terminated in a searing flash of destruction.

It was a fire that razed the apartment and burned up so much joy that awful day—just after our tenth wedding anniversary.

The fire was a visit in the silent hours of the night while we were at rest. My wife and I could only cart ourselves and our child away with only the clothes on our backs. It was like the biblical second coming of Christ. My handheld was another lucky survivor as it was with me before I started running barefoot into the darkness.

As I sat across the road, watching our apartment go up in flames, I was so taken aback I couldn't comprehend it was really happening—even knowing full well that it was. Both in shock and denial, I was hoping I could wake up and realize it was just a bad dream. At that very moment, it was impossible to imagine that any of our belongings would ever be replaced. I did thank God that I was alive and that my family was as well. If either of them had been lost, they could never have been replaced. It seemed the fire was burning inside me. I just couldn't let go of our life there and all those precious belongings.

A few days after the horrible incident, it occurred to me in the form of solace to reassure myself that this would not be the end of my family and me. I repeatedly said, "We've been through worse, and we will definitely overcome this." I didn't envisage the effect of the incident on me psychologically, so I didn't know the fire was only the beginning.

As the moon rose in the night sky, I couldn't fathom how much worse things would turn out to be. It was surprising that the loss of our possessions, gutted by fire, wouldn't be the most terrible thing of all. An electric spark from a neighbor's apartment was all it took. But it was going to be the aftermath that was going to be a fight to keep things under control. How were we to make financial decisions, where would we eat, when will the insurance company help us, and where would we find a new apartment? All these unanswered questions in the middle of being traumatized and exhausted.

And yet, the horror of our hellish experience was mixed with, and almost covered up by, the outpouring of kindness, support, and generosity from our community.

This began while our house was still in flames. The Red Cross came to our aid, taking us from the roadside to a nearby hotel. And we were there for the next eight weeks. It became our temporary home where we could catch our breath and make plans for resuscitation.

The morning after the fire I went to work and told my friends and colleagues of the horror. The message, like the fire, was spread around the school and released an avalanche of support, coupled with hugs and comforting words. Different people, in their own little ways, expressed concern; even students. Later that day I had an envelope full of checks and cash handed to me. Friends from my work and my wife's workplace gathered the next day to strategize how to meet our immediate, midterm and long-term needs.

Many checked on us throughout the time of rebuilding. Neighbors, some of which we barely knew, stopped over and handed us cash. Some offered furniture, clothes and even a place to stay. Far away friends and family called, sent care packages and wrote beautiful, loving cards and emails.

Despite our insurance and some little savings, the wait for things to normalize was still burdensome. I had no idea how slow and tedious the insurance process would be—nor how quickly we would exhaust our savings. It was a period of anxiety having to depend on and wait endlessly for the insurance settlement to come to our aid.

When we first moved to the hotel, we were just watching local TV without a good cable provider. Although we missed YouTube, and we weren't enjoying Netflix, we were lucky to have a place to live. However, Maria, her husband and child, our old neighbors, were not so lucky. They were sent to a shelter where there's essentially no privacy. In addition, the shelter was far from their jobs and their daughter's school. They couldn't afford to rent another apartment and they had no other options. They just had to wait until housing accommodates them. We often prayed for them to find an apartment so they could get their lives together again.

I knew my wife, son and I were blessed. We were surrounded by beautiful people, who out of their love-filled hearts, helped us deal with the situation. We were comforted by them with everything we needed including cash.

Now, I must say, if you have not been a victim of a devastating fire, and you are just reading to stay prepared, you can count your blessings. There are a few things you can learn to prepare yourself "just in case."

Such an instance of loss can be extremely traumatic. Even without the loss of lives or infliction of injuries, there is the likelihood of shock, disbelief, emptiness, anxiety, depression, a sense of loss, both of properties and self-esteem, and a host of others.

Unfortunately, when you least want to, you may have to make quick decisions on important life issues. It's hard to know what to do, who to call, where to start, at a time as this. Such situations can change your life depending on the choices you make. So, it is very important to know where to begin, who can help and how to start over.

If you have recently been a victim of such loss, try not to stress. I know it's not easy—but you have to try. Once you've started to recover emotionally, then responsively you will recover financially. The state of mind is most important.

This book is a simple, but I hope informative, guide on handling the aftermath of a domestic fire and can apply to any similar incidence of loss from dealing with your insurance claims to restoring damaged belongings and getting your life back. This book presents a range of practicalities, that we hope will help you through such a stressful time.

CHAPTER ONE : DEALING WITH LOSS

Truth be told, it isn't easy handling loss. However, there are always ways to help make recovery easier. Mental health support is needed right from the moment of the outbreak, even before the fire is put out. That's because the road of from shock to recovery is difficult and help is needed to prevent emotional breakdown as the victim travels.

Fire is known to be one of the most destructive disasters one can ever imagine happening because of its potency to raze within the twinkle of an eye. Its resultant effect will not only take a toll on finances, but also on the emotional state of its victims. There are always huge losses in fire disasters, ranging from personal possessions, to furniture, to important documents, to even the house itself, and the possibility of rendering the family homeless. Handling such losses becomes stressful from the thoughts about the loss of possessions as well as the loss of the very place you found comfort and called home every day. Let it be known that everyone that experiences large-scale fire damage goes through a period of grieving and a tough process of readjustment. Knowing the typical stages involved during this period and how to handle each, helps to endure the journey.

For all instances of loss, either of lives or properties, there are stages of grief that generally take place.

Shock is the first stage of grieving. Let's face it, no one ever plans to be caught in such a web of loss and confusion. At this stage, victims find it hard to comprehend the situation fully and at least, temporarily, become numb and disoriented. However, the initial shock is beneficial as it prevents the victims from taking on the full magnitude of the tragedy all at once.

As the shock wears off, the next stages that follow are anger, depression, and hopelessness. These reactions tend to alternate within the same period. Hence, they are not separated as completely unique stages. Depression from a major loss usually parades itself as anxiety, insomnia and crying, which can have a resultant effect on energy level and appetite. It can also make a person feel homeless because it happened so quickly and they're not immediately sure where they will stay. Some may get hung up on regrets and the "had I known" syndrome, especially since it is believed by many that it was preventable. Anger can also manifest itself between feelings of depression and hopelessness, and it can be directed at anyone who could be said to relate to the cause of the incident.

The last stage of loss and grief is acceptance, where one is finally able to accept that the deed's been done and there is no going back. At this point letting go of the anger and depression begins to take place and the possibility of hope and happiness is realized. Acceptance becomes much easier when a replacement for the major loss is found. As regards fire losses, most of which deal with the loss of the home, acceptance becomes easy after a new home is found and significant steps are taken to re-establish a normal life. *The earlier the replacement, the earlier the acceptance.*

The emotional state is of paramount importance because the ability to exercise correct judgment and forge ahead is largely dependent on the state of mind. Therefore, before concentrating on other areas of life, prompt attention should be given to the emotional state. If the mind is in a bad place, it will greatly affect the ability to handle things, thereby hindering the possibility of making progress.

CHAPTER TWO : MANAGING THE SITUATION

It's curious that we care less about the most important issue when dealing with the aftermath of a fire. We tend to put the cart before the horse by putting a premium on financial recovery over the state of mind of the victims. One is a factor while the other is a product of that factor. We tend to give attention to the product of the factor, rather than the factor itself. We fail to understand that, it takes a sound mind to make sound decisions that will assist the victims and help kick them back to life again. Psychologically, the mind is the powerhouse of our actions, and its state determines the quality of the actions we produce.

A disastrous fire could be so damaging to the mind, especially if there was a great loss. The suddenness of such disasters is shocking, which gives way to anger, depression, hopelessness and all manner of negative emotions.

It is very needful and helpful to be acquainted with how to manage such situations effectively. The reaction of the people involved, and how they handle the situation, goes a very long way to how long or short the process to acceptance will be. It is the determining factor as to whether the victim wants to remain depressed or wants a quick recovery. It determines whether the victim continues in loss or starts over to reacquire.

Another common mistake victims make is, continuing to live in the predicament, by being consumed by the anger and sadness they have just experienced. It can be so blinding that they forget to give time to taking proper care of themselves. It's like feeling sorry over the proverbial spilled milk.

However, it is expedient for anyone, in such a situation, to understand the importance of giving more attention to recovery than regrets. The following strategies can help victims have a better perspective of the situation and put them in an awesome position for recovery.

DON'T HOLD IN YOUR EMOTIONS— EXPRESS THEM

A loss is very painful, scary and unsettling. The emotions that come with it are so hard to process all at once. Hence, many resort to tamping it all down and ignoring their feelings. But that is more dangerous because unresolved grief eventually gets complicated thereby resulting in depression, anxiety, substance abuse, and ill health. Trying to ignore your pain or keep it from surfacing will only aggravate the problem in the long run. For a lasting solution and total healing of the mind, it is necessary to face your grief and purposefully deal with it. So, let it all out—cry, scream and vent as much as you need to. It's healthier than holding it in.

IT'S OKAY TO FEEL SAD

In today's society, we are encouraged to pretend and act like all is okay rather than face reality. We are encouraged to get up and dust it all off, put up a fine front, put on a clean shirt, and get back to life as quickly as possible. Just like that? The truth is, it doesn't work that way. Part of the process of recovery is the ability to give in to grief, pain or loss fully. Until then, it will be difficult to accept. You don't have to act like superman or woman. It's okay to express your emotions; it's okay to be real, it's okay to be sad. It doesn't make you less of a man or woman. So, be open about needing time to feel better, because the more honest you are about the loss, and the emotions that follow, the better your chances of recovery.

DON'T ISOLATE YOURSELF—SURROUND YOURSELF WITH PEOPLE WHO LOVE YOU

You may want to grieve privately , thereby staying away from your immediate environment and resorting to being alone. As much as that is okay to do, you should always get back to your normal circle of friends and family. You must let people in. Don't isolate yourself on the basis of passive aggression toward your immediate circle of contacts by staying away from them totally. People are part of your healing process, so it will be detrimental staying away from them. Spending time alone is actually fine, but isolation isn't a healthy way of dealing with loss. On your journey of healing, a friend, partner, confidant or spiritual leader can be of immense help. Allow loved ones and other close contacts to sympathize and empathize with you. Don't isolate yourself.

TAKE GOOD CARE OF YOURSELF

When your mind is filled with memories of your "used to be" home—eating and sleeping become a difficult thing to do. Whether you feel like it or not, you have to determine to eat enough, get plenty of rest, and do things that are soothing to you and make you comfortable. The truth is that the shock that comes as a result of loss has an intense effect on our emotional, mental, physical and spiritual well-being. The body needs food even during this time, to help give strength to handle the trauma. Self-care is critical! So, do things that the body needs; lots of warm baths, freshly pressed organic juices, exercising, homemaking, reading inspiring books, talking with friends, getting out in the sunshine, taking walks, and learning to nurture yourself. Figure out the things you need to be doing to stay healthy and go for them.

IF YOU MUST NUMB YOUR PAIN, CHOOSE POSITIVE THINGS

It's very important to note that numbing oneself with substances isn't helpful; it's disastrous. While substances such as drugs and alcohol may offer a temporary escape from painful thoughts, they eventually return greater and now complicated by the side effects of drugs and alcohol. And there is a great danger; the use of them can lead to addiction. Furthermore, they are destructive to health and well-being. So, rather than turning to short-term fixes, turn to healing, counseling, exercise, or volunteering. Those would be much better and more long-lasting. It might take a long while but trust that it's the better way to go. Understand the use of time. Time helps, time heals, take your time, don't boycott time. Though, time might not cure, might not take away all feelings of loss, it can make that acute and searing pain less intense, and that red-hot emotion can become less painful. Accepting and embracing your new "normal" life might also help reconcile losses.

ONLY YOU CAN TELL YOURSELF HOW TO FEEL

There is no "right" way to feel when one's home is turned into an inferno. We feel differently and therefore react in different ways to situations. You might fall out into crying hysterically, or you might become a "Mr. Bean," or you might laugh uncontrollably. Wherever you fall on the spectrum is fine regardless of how people interpret it. Do not let anyone tutor you on how to feel. Grieve your own loss in your own way, as long as it isn't detrimental to your health or harmful to others. Let yourself feel whatever you feel without embarrassment or judgment.

CHAPTER THREE : LIVING IN A SHELTER

Anyone displaced or rendered homeless, through any situation, could not be more pleased than to have a temporary place to lodge until everything is put in order again. They would definitely be satisfied with a room with at least a bed, cooking items, and a place to bathe. In a disruptive event all of these things, regardless of their size, would be so appreciated as long as it was affordable and legal. It would even be more thrilling if the place possessed a small yard for gardening. But if you can't afford it and you don't have a family that can assist you, your choices are seriously limited.

After the ordeal of losing a house and not having an alternative to replace it with, you might just want to have your head laid anywhere to sleep till you are reoriented. Many would be pleased with a decent sized room as long as it was legal and offered their essential needs. These temporary shelter arrangements might certainly not be the choice of the victim before now, and might not provide the optimum comfort they used to enjoy. However, in a crisis situation having such is a blessing, and it will be a thing of great delight if care and precautions are taken.

WHAT IS A SHELTER?

A shelter, according to this context, can be regarded as a place serving as temporary accommodation to assist those in need of it. It would typically include beds, a kitchen, showers, and sometimes, a place of worship, all usually in one room. Some are free, while moderate fees are charged by others.

There are also some regarded as emergency shelters. They only open when the temperature is below freezing. Anyone who needs shelter can utilize either of the two.

Shelters are mainly for the displaced. If they weren't made available, we would have many more people on the streets. Shelters provide varying experiences depending on the environment of the particular location, noting that the inhabitants reflect the environment. There are some that are pretty nice with large dormitories. One could be so lucky to have access to good bunk beds, a large bathroom with plenty of sinks, toilets, urinals, big courtyards to hang out in, medical care, legal advice, a psychiatrist, or even more, a barber. The food is generally not up to standard, but some groups may come in and serve home-cooked meals on the weekends. This isn't applicable to all shelters. Acceptance might not be coming from everyone around as some staff could be rude, but definitely, there are always good ones you might meet and would want to meet again.

TYPES OF SHELTERS

- **Regular, Generic Homeless Shelters**

   This type caters to all—that is: men, women and children. Generally, one can be accommodated for a maximum of two weeks, which is the waiting period before you get your first check from insurance or the government depending on the type of calamity. If you don't have a job generating money to pay for shelter, then the feasibility of retaining the shelter is not assured. It's worth doing research beforehand, so you can be prepared in the event that you need this kind of help.

   The quality of these shelters vary, and this relates to the building itself, the accommodations, the staff and the services rendered.

- **Women's Shelters**

   These are solely created to shelter women. They contain the same attributes of homeless shelters as stated above but with additional considerations for women. Most of these do not disclose the location because many of the women are escaping abusive husbands or dangerous living conditions. One of the primary purposes of this type of shelter is protection since most of the women sheltered there are victims of battering, marital abuse, rape, and similar circumstances. Therefore, their privacy is enforced. The restrictions of these types of shelters can be somewhat burdensome but they are put in place for the safety of the women using the shelter.

There have been some cases where people have lied to get into some of these shelters because they are usually a step above other homeless shelters in service.

- **Recovery Shelter**

Some recovery shelters are set up with a drug and alcohol rehab program. The occupants of these shelters are provided with beds each night though the room will have to be shared with others.

Men and women accommodated here are all housed in the same building. It operates like a rehab. The sheltered must attend a nightly routine of education five days a week. The classes are focused on the following: substance abuse education, relapse prevention, safety seeking, and cognitive behavioral therapy. These occupants are separated into rooms on the basis of gender. There are a specific number of people per room, and there is a common area used by all.

Each night, the occupants are served meals, prepared by a chef, using food from local food banks,. Clothing and items needed for hygiene are usually donated to the shelter.

A medical professional comes twice a week to provide

medications for overall health and , methadone for those trying to get clean. This program is known as medication-assisted treatment services. Also, a weekly AA meeting is held in one of the conference rooms.

HOW SHELTERS WORK

Shelters are very different from one area to another. Generally the first stop is an assessment shelter. That is where the plan for the individual or family is determined. If all you need is a place to rest, you may stay there indefinitely. Others will be assigned to a "permanent" shelter. Actually, the permanent shelter isn't in the real sense "permanent" but in context, because it isn't the assessment shelter. It is more like a 6-12 month allotment until you get a more permanent place you can move to. Or you may be assigned to another shelter for an additional 6-12 month period.

It's important to know that you must dial 311, to let them know you want to go to a homeless intake center. You will be provided with the location and how to get there. They will send a van to transport you if you are too far away to walk.

Advantages of a normal shelter include; privacy, a place to keep your belongings, a safe place from potential aggressors and a place to get together with family and friends.

In a shelter, an intake officer takes you to a room where you are extensively interviewed. Your interview consists of obtaining biographical data, medical history and if you are drug or alcohol dependent. They may also ask for your license or ID. Some shelters turn you away if you are unable to provide the information required.

The staff goes over the rules for the shelter and gives you a quick tour of the facility. You will also be provided with names and phone numbers of other agencies in the area that might be helpful to you.

- **Sleeping Arrangements**

  After approval, you are assigned to a room. You will be provided with a shower. Which, depending on the shelter, you might have to shower in front of others (of the same gender), with a time limit of 5-10 minutes to shower.

  After eating, you prepare to go to bed. The staff supplies you with blankets, sheets and a pillow. Generally upper or lower bunks are available to choose from.

- **In the Morning**

  By morning, the day staff will have come in. You are given between your waking time to 7 am to change out of your nightclothes, brush your teeth, do your hair/makeup, and be out of the door. Failure in any these area can cause you to lose your shelter privileges. You place your bedding in a large receptacle at the front of the room for it to be washed. Feel free to ask the staff if you aren't sure where to put it.

You will be assigned a locker where you can keep all of your other belongings. They remain there until you are leaving the shelter. You can spend your day however you like, but you must be back by 7 pm or you will lose your place. Always notify the staff, as soon as possible, if you won't be able to make it back in time. Only important reasons are acceptable, such as a medical emergency or work scheduling conflict and the like. They may be willing/able to assist you. But note that the shelter isn't staffed between 7 am and 4:30 pm. That is how the shelters work.

HOW DO YOU LIVE IN A SHELTER?

The sole purpose of creating shelter is to help people. They are mostly managed by good people who truly care and want to help. You can always be comfortable there till you get a new place to live, you only need to know how best to live there.

It could be terrible at times, living in a homeless shelter, having to live with strangers, and be anxious about cold or hot weather. Not knowing what you will do in the future can make you anxious, but the shelter is there to help.

At times, and in various locations, there had been reports of crime, over crowdedness, and even the transmission of disease. These situations are normally reacted to and rectified so you can still consider a shelter a great place to get started again.

You will have to live with people from diverse backgrounds and personalities. Most aren't quiet and friendly, rather you may find gossips, cliques, bullies, thieves, drug addicts, and the like. But you can also meet good people with positive attitudes as well. Time in a shelter is always memorable, especially if you are a humorous person and can get along with other people.

Issues like theft may arise, you being the victim. Staff may complain about sanitation or a fellow resident. There might be too many restrictive rules and regulations, but trust me, all of this wouldn't stop you from appreciating your stay at the shelter.

The fear of being labeled a "snitch" has made people afraid to report others' behaviors, thereby making actions like robberies, assaults, and even rape go unpunished, and sometimes increase. You will be saving yourself from unnecessary trouble if you conduct yourself well, and don't mix with the wrong set of people, or talk about other people's issues. It is often better to keep to one's self. Avoid fights, keep control of your temper as you may likely want to flare up from people's actions, especially when they act like they are better than you.

In most shelters, they would like to know if you have been proactively trying to acquire a more permanent shelter. You are required to fill out worksheets with apartment or other housing contact information.

THE FOODS

Apart from the pleasure of movies and other programs watched from a big screen TV, there is access to a fridge stocked full of food donated from local eateries that guests can choose from any time. This might be a service exclusively by good shelters. Being filled already with sandwiches and burritos can make you skip dinner.

There is generally a buffet service provided by soup kitchens that serve two meals a week to anyone who shows up. You can pile and cart away as much as you like. Goodies like pastries and cups of noodles are often available as well. Some shelters host different volunteer groups on certain days, which provide meals—things like pizza or barbecue. Provisions are also made for vegetarian meals, at some shelters.

RULES AND REGULATIONS OF A SHELTER

Shelters might not be and are indeed not the best of places compared to one's home, but they are blessings for anyone who needs them. Any guest at a shelter will be doing him/herself a huge favor by carefully abiding by the rules to ensure having a place to stay until ready to move.

Every shelter has certain rules, and many explicitly forbid the smuggling in of substances like drugs, weapons, or even being under the influence of them. Most times, cops are let in at nights. They ask for name, address, ID, etc. from everyone. If it is suspected that you are under an influence, or you are holding stuff, you are removed and either taken to the police station or to the hospital.

The shelters are constructed in a way that makes all your activities open to staff and residents; there are usually no stall doors. This is to avoid activities that contravene the shelter. The use of a cellphone in dorms is not allowed, due to issues in time past of sharing inappropriate pictures of other residents. It is therefore limited and can be in use outside of dorms, like the smoking area and garage.

Most shelters believe in their own system of helping you structure your life better. Therefore, some enforce ridiculous curfews. This doesn't go well with most people, so you can always "apply for an extension." Keep your possessions in a locker. Do not leave anything unattended to.

CHAPTER FOUR : SIMPLE RECOVERY STEPS

After the effect of a serious loss on a person's mental health has been dealt with, the next thing to attend to is its physical implications. As soon as the fire brigade completes their assignment and leaves, the house itself becomes your responsibility. Moving on might seem almost impossible, but trust me, it doesn't have to be. It is expedient to know how and where to start handling it, and this makes it easier to get through.

The following steps would be very helpful in your physical recovery process:

CONTACT YOUR INSURANCE COMPANY OR INSURANCE BROKER

Your first step should be contacting your insurance company or insurance broker to file your claim. The sooner you start that process, the sooner you will receive the help you need. Expediting your claim can shorten the time until you can begin repairs or search for a new apartment. Many insurance carriers also provide help for daily expenses during such circumstances; this is known as "loss of use funds." They can also help with finding cleaning or abatement services.

Before any major clean-up has been carried out, the insurance company may send out a claim form and arrange for a claims adjuster to inspect the damage. However, in order to prevent further damage to the property, you are permitted to carry out emergency work. If you will not be able to occupy the house, try as much as possible to protect valuables and personal affects.

SEE IF YOU HAVE A RENTER'S INSURANCE

As a landlord, there is a need for protection from financial loss from damages to rental properties. This is provided by a landlord's insurance policy which covers property owners renting out residential homes, apartments, or condos. You are provided with help to cover the loss of income during periods that your rental units become uninhabitable due to circumstances beyond your control.

Depending on the insurance company and the options chosen you must find out what you are entitled to. A tenant also needs renter's insurance rather than solely depending on the landlord because the landlord's insurance policies do not cover tenant's belongings, no matter how damaged or destroyed. The tenant can only be compensated when the landlord is sued for the damage, especially if it happened due to his negligence. And in such case, the liability portion of the landlord's policy would have to pay the legal fees and any other settlements.

FIND AND PROTECT YOUR VALUABLES

To prevent further loss or damage to a property, the insurer usually asks that preventive measures be taken, such as necessary repairs. Many household policies have an emergency response service that helps in such situations.

All doors, windows and other forms of entry should be secured against unauthorized access. If the damage is noticed at the roof or staircase, don't go in until it's checked by a building contractor and made safe. There might be need to cover the roof with a tarpaulin or remove and secure loose materials.

Employ a contractor if the building needs to be boarded up. It will help to safeguard against unauthorized entry or any liability for injury or damage to third parties. The costs and expenses should be covered by the insurance policy. Ensure the police are informed if the house would be left unoccupied. It is also advisable to empty water tanks, especially during winter to avoid damage by freezing.

TEMPORARY STORAGE FOR UNDAMAGED ITEMS

If the damage was partial and deemed safe to re-enter the house, go in and remove anything that wasn't affected by the fire. It is also recommended that such items are cleaned after being removed. Try securing and saving undamaged possessions because you might not be able to leave them in the house while repairs are going on. Before committing to such costs, check to see if they are covered by your policy with the insurance company or claims assessor.

SEEK ALTERNATIVE ACCOMMODATION

If the abode is not habitable, then there is a need to make plans for alternative accommodation. This could mean staying with friends or relatives, or a hotel or hostel for a few days while seeking a more permanent place to stay while repairs are being carried out. Also, check your insurance policy to see if it covers the cost of alternative accommodation before you book or rent anywhere. It may cover for the period of ongoing repair, and it's usually limited to a percentage of the building or value of contents insured. IF YOU ARE RENTING, THE INSURANCE MAY NOT COVER YOU, BUT THE REDCROSS CAN BE VERY HELPFUL.

Contact any estate or real estate agent for professionals that specialize in accommodations in your area. Read the ads for apartments and houses for rent in the local newspapers.

REACH OUT TO YOUR LOCAL DISASTER RELIEF AGENCY

It is terrifying to witness a house fire, especially for children,. If immediate assistance is needed for shelter, food or other personal needs, or if staying at a hotel or with friends or relatives isn't available, reach out to your local disaster relief agency like the Red Cross or Salvation Army. Many times, these organizations can provide temporary shelter, food or other personal needs for free.

Even if it's only for a night, find a safe and comfortable place to relocate, this will help plan your next steps, and give time for the family to rest and recover.

CONTACT YOUR LOCAL LAW ENFORCEMENT AGENCY

Looters and squatters can be attracted to locations even such as an empty home with fire damage. Your property can be secured during your absence if you alert your local police. Boarding up windows and doors will be an addition to security. This could be done yourself or by hiring a professional. Also, before commencing the job, check with the fire department to ensure the house is safe to enter.

CONTROL YOUR FINANCES

Regardless of your situation, financial responsibilities are like the clock, it keeps on going. You are therefore advised to prepare with an insurance company that covers mortgages, and probably other recurring costs like car payments. And since you won't be in your home, it will be economical to cancel cable, internet and other ongoing services accounts. Keep your receipts when replacing the items to ensure you are quickly reimbursed.

MAKE A LIST OF DAMAGED ITEMS

Make a list of all the items that were lost or damaged in the fire to ensure you are reimbursed properly. Information like make, model, serial numbers, and receipts will be required by your insurer. This might be a difficult thing to do if the house was totally destroyed or can't be accessed, but you can present a proof of purchase and exact costs by searching online bank statements on your computer. Lists of important documents that were lost in the fire such as licenses, birth certificates, passports, titles and deed's, medical records, tax information, etc., should be made so that they can be replaced immediately. Your agent would let you know the required items for your claim. It is wise to be proactive. Many insurance companies suggest that you videotape the contents of your home or apartment, so you have proof of the existence of items that were lost. You can make a major video the first time and then just update to add new items added after the original video was made.

CHECK ON THE SAFETY OF YOUR HOME

House fires can disfigure your home and cause it to lose its beauty and structural integrity. In addition, it can leave behind noxious fumes from burned materials. Always wait until a fire marshal has confirmed the area is safe before going in if you need to return home to recover items. Aside from the fact that it is dangerous, it can void parts of your insurance policy, which might affect your reimbursement. So you only return, for any reason, when it is confirmed safe by the fire department and your insurer.

WAIT TO TURN ON UTILITIES

To prevent further damage, the fire department will turn off utilities in some cases. Be sure you contact them and your utility provider before turning them on again. The connection of unsafe utilities can again result in fires, gas leaks, and severe water damage. So, have the home inspected by a professional before turning on your utilities.

CHAPTER FIVE: BEFORE YOU START OVER

There needs to be a correct perspective on certain things before one can successfully start over. One needs to be placed in a position of strength psychologically. You must be able to truthfully provide answers to some important questions. Questions you need to ask yourself. By doing so, you can prepare not only your own mind but also that of your wife and kids for the journey ahead. Some of the things that need to be handled with a proper perspective include:

GOD IS NOT PUNISHING ME BY BURNING DOWN MY HOUSE

Many are of the belief that when such disasters like fire razing a house, it's a sign of God's displeasure towards the person. Most Christians have been faced with the question of why bad things happen and have been fed with several religious answers which never satisfy the skeptic or serious student of the Word of God. The reason being that they don't portray the true character of God. God's character is said to be good and nothing short of good. He isn't bipolar and therefore not two-sided. Moreover He doesn't change or waver. So, any theory, belief or perception that terms Him as wicked or evil isn't portraying Him accurately.

How do I imagine such a father, and He is said to be our Father, and definitely even the best man on earth can't be better than God. How then do we ascribe properties we can't even ascribe to a good man, to a good God? The goodness of God should be the foundation and basis of our theology, for it is what He came to demonstrate in Christ. Scripture tells us that "God is Love." *Whoever does not love does not know God, because God is love.* (1 John 4:8)

When we are filled with the idea that God is always good and loves us unconditionally, come what may, then expectation meets our experience. That simple shift in the mind produces a remarkable way of life because it realigns us with God's eternal kingdom which depicts love. By then, we begin to operate from a perspective of abundance and favor, instead of that of poverty and struggle. The calamities that befall man are better seen as the result of the imperfect state of the world as we now know it. The consequences of living in a "fallen" world, simply create cause and effect. One thing we must never do is listen to those who make us have a wrong notion about the nature of God, because resting in the true nature of God is the basis of how believers live. Knowing the nature of God, as trivial as it may seem, is very important in the state of the world because the absence of the knowledge of the love of God is the reason many cannot and will not love. We produce the very acts we think of God, and how we position ourselves in this also impacts our perspective on this thing we call life.

God did not burn your house down. Unfortunately, we have an enemy who comes to steal, kill and destroy, and that is not God. Rather, God's purpose is that we have a richly satisfying life. God loves you way beyond human understanding. Let your faith remain in His love for you, and know that even in terrible circumstances, it is not His will, and He is not happy you are there, but He is with you to help you get up and even get up better.

It is challenging to find meaning in a tragedy. Being in a state of despair challenges you to cling to your faith in God's love, grace, and mercy. If you live thinking God is behind your calamity, you tend to accept things or give up because you fall into hopelessness and in that condition you will not forge ahead.

YOUR CHILDREN ARE ALSO AFFECTED BY THE LOSS

Children have been known to experience many kinds of losses, but not all are tragic. Many can't be differentiated from their normal life cycle transitions, beginning with birth. Our coming into the world was through a major loss, that is, the rupture of our state of biological oneness with our mothers, and afterward, we need healing. During infancy and throughout the first year of life, children need their parents to provide lots of physical touching, feeding and nurturing, so they can develop a solid sense of attachment, and human value. They need to experience love.

There is need to help children deal with loss; whether it be as a result of normal transitions like adjusting to a move or a new baby in the family, or more serious losses. They need to be taught the basic lessons of the heart. And in order to do this effectively, our own minds and hearts must be examined as well.

Our first responsibility is to have our own emotional house in order. By so doing, we will be attentive and also creative in our response to children, thereby helping them deal with the circumstances. Otherwise, we will only be vulnerable, block them from being open to us, over-identify with them and lose a sense of appropriate boundaries. We actually can't take away someone else's pain, not even that of a child, but we shouldn't be restrained from reaching out to them non the less. Nothing is as potent as love.

In conclusion, we should note that children, just like we do, have feelings and needs and are therefore affected by any form of loss that hits them. Also, they have far fewer resources and abilities to cope than we have, therefore we, regardless of our own helplessness, must help them.

YOUR SEX LIFE CAN BE AFFECTED, SO YOU SHOULD TAKE CARE
Studies have shown that heightened levels of cortisol can have a negative effect on the sex drive, making us too preoccupied to relax and be in the mood. Experts also state that hormone responses in the body can be changed by feelings of depression thereby lowering the desire for sex and intimacy. And this can be a blow to a relationship. All energy is needed

and must be used in order to start over and recover that which was lost. Research also has it that couples who have regular sex are happier and feel better about their personal selves and their significant others.

For a successful long-term relationship, a regular physical desire for each other is necessary. However, it can be affected by the smallness of the new accommodation and the absence of privacy. Disturbances and interruptions from the children can also be a hindrance. Sex life suffers, then starves if the accommodations are not suitable for the whole family. Knowing all this, it is then your responsibility to save your sex life and prevent it from being destroyed by the house fire. It will be more disastrous if you let the pain and anxiety of the loss take hold of your whole being. So, get to the root, handle it, attend to the problem, know how to create time and privacy for that purpose. You will be happier, more relaxed, more alert, and more energized to start over.

CHAPTER SIX : STARTING OVER

Starting over would definitely be a nice thing to do, wouldn't it? How nice will it be to get a clean slate or a second chance? It's very natural to think about shaking off and forging ahead after a devastating occurrence. But the truth is, it isn't an easy task for anyone. There is no easy way to start over, whether after a failed relationship, loss of property, end of a career, loss of a loved one, or any unprecedented destabilizing situation. To buckle under the weight of the blow can feel like our only option.

A loss is always painful, no matter how it seems, and it can also be costly regarding time, money, energy or all three. We must always understand that loss is part of life. It can't be avoided. It's surprising how most people don't talk about their losses, failures of mistakes and you wonder if they never faced any, like their lives were all rosy. They'll tell you about a new car just bought, about a new apartment, and positive things of that sort. Not about how the company went into bankruptcy. Not how their marriage ended in divorce.

When you study the lives of great people, you will know most of them had to pull through their darkest hours to be where they are today. Their stories have taught us that many great things didn't succeed the first time. One thing was always clear about them; repeated failures, losses, falls, frustrations, criticisms, and self-doubts before eventually rising to achieve greatness. You may not be a reading fan of the author of 'Harry Potter'; J.K Rowling's books, but she is someone who had once had the urge to commit suicide but pulled through and persisted. Her success story of today is one that speaks of over 400million books sold, countless licensing deals, and at one point was the second richest woman in the UK, after the Queen. This is someone that has once contemplated taking her own life, so hard to imagine, but that's the reality. Talk of Job in the Bible, talk of how he lost everything he ever had; from his properties to his children, then his health but he never gave up and was blessed by God for his resilience with a double fold abundance of all that he lost. Talk of

Edison, who failed 10,000 times before hitting it at last on an electric lightbulb. He was made to go through 9,999 start overs before he eventually produces that which made his name indelible, not only in history but in the hall of fame.

We are not praying not to face all or any of these but admonishing us on the need to be proactive when such arise, rather than stick ours head in the sand, wishing it never happened.

The following are seven effective and time-tested steps to take while starting over:

FORGIVE YOURSELF FOR WHAT HAPPENED

While this can take time, remember that forgiveness is not only for others, as you need to forgive yourself, too. You have to let go, and be easy on yourself, if in any way you blame yourself and feel there was probably a way you could have prevented the incident. You have to do yourself that favor and forgive yourself. Make a deliberate choice to let go of the hurt, anger, resentment, or pain you think your own actions caused you. Feeling guilty for your mistake or negligence will do you no good other than to enslave you to the past and hinder you from starting over, much less moving forward. You need no formal way to forgive yourself. There is no special ceremony required for this, other than to just let go of the pain you feel.

FORGET THE PAST AND FOCUS ON THE FUTURE

The quicker you leave your past behind and forget your loss, the quicker it will be to embrace success by starting over. You can't forge ahead if you don't let go of the past. Let past be past, bygone be bygone, just as the water flows under a bridge and is gone. Since you can't change what happened, you can focus on rewriting, amending and getting better. Why then wouldn't you stop worrying about it? Take stock of your lessons learned, repackage your knowledge, experience and skills and move on to accomplish your purpose.

You will have to eliminate anything that keeps holding you back if you truly want to march on. Find even the smallest ways to move on if you don't want to get stuck in the past.

TAKE WHATEVER HAPPENED AS AN OPPORTUNITY TO DO BETTER

It is often said that whatever doesn't kill you, makes you stronger. Challenges, when handled positively, make us better for it. Starting over can be a way of sloughing off what didn't work. It can also be a way of stomping out fears you've seen were unnecessary. Being able to do any of these things makes one a more disciplined, optimistic, godly, inspiring, and financially intelligent individual. Always remember that no matter what life throws at you, you alone have the power to say, "This can make me better, not bitter."

We may feel bad, and therefore shy away from our losses, failures or defeat, but they are opportunities for us to rewrite our stories and inspire others on to victory. There is no victory without a war. We can't have one without the other. To be great in life, to eventually be regarded as a winner, we need to fight, we only need the courage to keep fighting and moving forward.

THINK OF THIS FRESH START AS A TIME OF HEALING

Always refer to this fresh start as a process of healing when talking to yourself or others about it. It could be termed financial or emotional healing. There is a kind of soothing, uplifting, nurturing and loving energy in the word healing, that positively influences your attitude and experience.

PUT ON YOUR HEART OF BRAVERY

Most times, starting over involves taking a risk. This is normal, and usually difficult, especially when you've given your all and invested everything into something, and it turns out to be a loss. Dealing with it forces you to face the uncertainties of starting over knowing it could turn out better or even worse than the former. That's why it's always harder to move on than to hold on. But you will have to take a brave leap in order to pursue something more meaningful. Playing safe, or posing a nonchalant attitude is never enough to make significant shifts in a situation.

SHARPEN YOUR SWORD OF RESILIENCE

Rather than play the blame game, it will require a lot from you to start over and reach the goal of settling down comfortable again in your own apartment or home. Our normal physical, mental or emotional self isn't so abreast with this route, but it is required of us to suppress it and restrain these forces. It takes a lot of resilience in us to keep striving to achieve our goals, even when everything around us is chanting 'stop.' Resilience is the motivation that keeps us going not minding discomfort and discouragement. Discouragement can even be from close associates, but resilience helps to keep fighting on. This mindset of resilience helps return one to a former state of strength, health, and success no matter how bad the situation might seem.

PUT ON YOUR CLOAK OF DEDICATION AND PERSISTENT COMMITMENT

Change doesn't just come by wishes, it responds to persistent commitment to effect the desired change. A faint heart finds it impossible to start over because it will eventually give up at the challenges and accept whatever comes its way. It requires continuous forward movement even when you feel all options have been exhausted, it requires making that one more phone call, attending one or more meeting(s), applying for one more loan, visiting one more office, waiting once more for that response from the insurer, just that final push which is often what is needed to make the difference. And this requires commitment and motivation, focus, and proactivity.

BE PATIENT WITH THE PROCESS

The consideration of time as a factor cannot be overemphasized, especially when it comes to starting all over. Change is always concerning time. Therefore, one needs to be realistic and so away with any form of the idea of jumping overnight from a shambled house to a new one. Intermediate steps most often will be necessary. For example, you might have to wait a while for the insurance company to conclude their investigation before handing you the money. It might also be necessary to work toward obtaining funds from other avenues if you were not insured, or the policy didn't cover all damages, and this requires time. Estimating a realistic time frame prevents frustration when progress takes longer than hoped.

Failure, defeat, or loss should be our teacher, not our undertaker!

Those things may delay us, but they mustn't defeat us. They can be described as temporary detours on the way, not dead-end streets. Loss checks in on one's ego and arrogance. It also helps us to identify true friends. It also helps to reevaluate the important things in our lives. It reveals our true character, where you get to meet the real you. Most challenges come in stages that cannot be skipped, they are school classes we have to learn from, and the inability to grow through them might lead to facing them over and over again. Some people never even venture into anything for not being able to handle defeat, failure or loss. This would definitely result in nothing. Action and reaction are equal and opposite. Nothing can happen without action. It's all about taking risks.

A ball gathers momentum once it starts rolling. Same as starting over. Once you see out, you will be faced with opportunities and eventually get to your destination. Let it be known that no matter how old you are, where you are in the world, how devastating your experience has been— you can start over. So, start now; there is no time to waste.

CHAPTER SEVEN : TACKLING THE CLEANUP

Looking at the building as a whole for cleanup will be intimidating and possibly overwhelming. It should be tackled one room at a time.

Disinfect after cleaning to kill the germs and suppress the smell left by the smoke.

It is always advisable to leave the scene intact for as long as possible until an inspection is made by the insurance company. Insurance is the single most important component in your recovery process, and this is why your broker or claims assessor has to be called immediately after the incident.

You may have signed up for two separate policies, one for the building, the other ensures the contents, and this may be issued differently by different companies. Contact them both.

> ➢ Claims Adjusters: Investigation will be carried out on behalf of your insurance company, by a firm of claims adjusters appointed to also deal with your insurance claim. They may wish to inspect the premises before you move or dispose of anything.

Try to be in agreement with the claims adjuster on the scope of the loss on what can be disposed of, salvaged or inspected by a specialist. Failure to agree with the claims adjuster before disposing of or moving any item may make you forfeit your claims at the negotiation stage. The claims adjuster wouldn't file your claim. It is your responsibility. Therefore you might need to contact builders, tradesmen, suppliers, and other professionals in the required fields to provide estimates for repairs or replacements.

Receipts for any emergency expenses incurred as a result of the fire should also be included. They will have to wait till you submit your full claim details, then a settlement offer will be made based on what they think is the reasonable value of your loss. You might lose your entitlements if you are not familiar with the scope of coverage included in the various clauses or extensions in the policy.

➤ Claims Assessors: You might need to appoint a claims assessor or contact your broker. A claims assessor helps in the entire inventory and negotiation process. They can document and cost the extent of repair or replacement. They help not only to estimate the cost but also carry out all necessary negotiations with the claims adjuster to ensure you are given all your entitled to under the policy. Inventory will be made on damaged personal property showing in detail, the quantity, description, amount of damage sustained, and the cost of repair or replacement. Any bill or document that will also help establish the item's value will be included in the inventory. Claims assessors usually charge a percentage of the settlement amount. And this is usually justified in the professional service delivered because they know what you are entitled to. They are conversant with such situations and know how best to handle them. They know exactly what the claims adjuster requires. If necessary, they can also supervise the repair work. They act exclusively on your behalf and give you the support, advice, and confidence needed to recover. They help to hasten the process, help get a reasonable settlement amount for you, ease your stress, and all these justify their appointment. You can also collaborate with contractors, that will do the work, without having to depend on them to produce written estimates.

➤ Inventory of Damage: The inventory process may seem difficult and upsetting. However, take the necessary time to ensure a complete inventory and estimate. You should inspect the damaged area carefully, but it is also important to avoid unnecessary delay. Nevertheless, do not overlook anything. You will not be paid for anything you did not claim. You might be provided with inventory forms by your insurer or claims assessor to help organize the job. Photographs might be a more convincing record of specific damage. Receipts for expenses like alternative accommodation, materials, labor and equipment rental should be kept.

> Reaching an Agreement: It is always understood by insurers in most cases that people might not be able to provide receipts for all damaged items, as it might have been destroyed by the fire. Nonetheless, an agreement about the value of damages is made between the insurer and the insured. If during the claims adjustment process, this is not achieved, provision is made in the policy for the appraisal of goods and the arbitration of differences. Some policies provide the insurer with options of whether to repair or replace, whichever is less. Many policies are on a "New for Old" basis, so if an item is damaged beyond repair, it should be replaced.

TACKLING THE CLEANUP

After the insurance company has been involved in all the required processes, the next thing is clean up. During this, ensure you are always protected by wearing surgical or rubber gloves and a mask if necessary, throughout the cleanup operation. Thoroughly wash hands with soap and water often, especially before handling food. If possible, use an anti-bacterial soap on your hands and avoid biting nails. Using two buckets, one filled with the cleaner, the other with plain water, keeps most of the dirty rinse water out of your solution. First, rinse out the sponge, mop or cleaning cloth you are using, in the water, wring it as dry as possible and keep it rolled up tight as you put it in the bucket containing cleaner. Frequently replace the rinse water.

> ➤ Water Damage: The premises might have been filled with a lot of water from the firemen's hoses. Dehumidifiers will remove moisture from the atmosphere. The premises will need to be thoroughly heated and ventilated, with the windows open, for several days. This will also help to remove odors. Also, consider security when that is being done. Do not use Liquefied Petroleum Gas heaters, because they create additional water vapor.

> ➤ Smoke Damage: More damage is caused by smoke than by fire itself. Smoke penetrates the most inaccessible spaces, and leaves behind, stains that are difficult to clean. Every smoke-damaged part of the premises should be thoroughly washed and disinfected. Destroyed items that need to be disposed of don't need washing; there is no point in cleaning them. If discovered after cleaning, that any item has not been satisfactorily cleaned, such item should be brought to the notice of the claims adjuster immediately. You may need to employ a contract cleaning company that specializes in post-fire restoration. But in cases where the smoke damage isn't severe, you may do it yourself. You can make use of regular household cleaning products; they will be efficient enough if used correctly. You can always check the label on the products for how to use, and how much to use. Some products are exclusively for some materials, that if used on any other material, will damage the material. The label will guide on that. Follow the directions and precautions on the container.

WALLS AND CEILINGS

Specialist advice is needed to remove soot and smoke from walls and ceilings. Sometimes, the severity of the smoke and heat may be too much to the extent of damaging the plasterboard, needing it to be stripped off and replaced. It can be separated from the brick or block with a hard wall plaster, and you will hear a hollow sound when you knock on the plaster. Until the walls and ceilings are completely dry, do not repaint.

CARPETS AND FLOORING

Carpet, lino, vinyl floor coverings might need to be replaced because they do not react well to water. If a carpet isn't severely damaged, it can be cleaned with a wet or dry vacuum cleaner. You can hire that from carpet stores, dry cleaning shops or tools rental companies. But note that, carpet usually shrinks after getting wet and might need to be thrown away. A piece of any discarded floor covering should be kept so as to show it to claims adjusters to tell its value.

By sanding and varnishing, you can sometimes restore original floorboards, which are tough and grooved, provided they haven't been scorched or warped. You can also treat semi-solid flooring the same way, but they are more susceptible to warping. Laminate floors will start to lip at the joins between boards; they are very prone to water damage. It is also advised that you treat floorboards and joists underneath for wood-rot and insecticide if floors have been exposed to water because the moisture level will make it conducive to mold and rot. And if not treated, it could seriously affect the structure of the house, by having long-term effects on it.

CLEANING SUPPLY CHECKLIST

The following are the basic needs, though not the complete list, required for cleaning the house: brushes, mops, buckets, hose, rubber gloves, cloths, cleaners, disinfectants, lubricating oil and garden refuse sacks.

CHAPTER EIGHT : DEALING WITH THE NEW YORK HOUSING AUTHORITY

It can be a trying time for anyone having his/her house razed by fire, resulting in damage of goods and properties, and emotional stability. The Red Cross can be of help by providing the family with a hotel for a few nights after which the Housing Authority of the city or state can offer temporary housing nearby, while repairs are going on. This is a standard procedure.

If you live in the USA, the different Housing Authority of each state can help get an apartment, but certain things are required to be fulfilled before getting the apartment. There is more probability of getting the house faster if you have income and can afford to pay the rent. Since there's also a high probability that you may not have enough to afford it as a result of the present loss. Your best chance then at securing an apartment would be to go for cheap accommodations.

WHAT IS THE NEW YORK HOUSING AUTHORITY?

The truth is that it is incredibly expensive to get market-rate apartments in most states and cities. For instance, only a small percentage of rental apartments are priced at the normal market rate. Thousands and millions of rental units that are subjected one way or the other to the regulation of subsidy are created by states and cities. There are a lot of cheap apartments out there, but it can be difficult to get one.

A typical Housing Authority is a public housing agency that participates in public housing programs. It is challenging to get safe, decent and affordable housing, so such agencies have placed it upon themselves to meet this challenge in comprehensive and innovative ways.

The New York City Housing Authority (NYCHA) is burdened with the mission of increasing opportunities for low and moderate New Yorkers by providing safe, affordable housing and facilitating access to social and community services. NYCHA's 328 public housing developments across New York City's five boroughs are being occupied by over 400,000 New Yorkers. Through NYCHA-administered Section 8 Leased Housing Program, another 235,000 receive subsidized rental assistance in private homes.

The Authority is the largest public housing authority (PHA) in North America. Experts consider it to be the most successful big-city public housing authority in the country. Whereas most large public housing authorities in the United States have demolished their high-rise projects and, in most cases, have them replaced them with lower scale housing, while New York's housing continues to be fully occupied. Most of its market-rate housing is also in high-rise buildings.

It is not easy getting into these facilities in New York, and in most cities, because incumbent residents are more focused on by the authority to protect them, and in some cases, give them huge discounts to advertise rents, while supply is restricted, thereby making it difficult for new people to form households. Occasionally though, new tenants get into subsidized or regulated housing and achieve real savings. Here's a guide on how you can try:

PUBLIC HOUSING

A housing subsidy can be granted to eligible low-income families, the elderly, and people with all types of disabilities. You will have to fill out and submit an application if you want to be considered for an apartment in a public housing development. You, as an applicant, are provided with the opportunity of selecting a first and a second borough choice, and filling in information about your total household income, family composition, current living situation, etc.

Specifically, the following is the list of documents required for the interview:

1. Marriage Certificate

2. Birth Certificate for everyone that will live with you

3. Social security information for everyone

4. Verification of immigration status

5. Proof of present address for the past three months.

6. Proof of rent payment/utility bills

7. Information about the landlord/owner

8. Documents showing family income in the last 12 months, social security income, SSI Awards letter, SSA/Benefit/Public assistance, income/food stamps/employment(pay stubs, and W2 forms, employment certification

9. Documents showing assets for the last 12 months, bank books, verification of other interest/dividend income, dividend, stock broker summary statement of stocks, bonds, or mutual funds. Copy of stock certificates or bonds.

10. Declaration of assets

11. Authorization for the release of information /privacy notice act

12. Social security number disclosure form

13. Verification of citizenship/eligible immigration status

14. Eligibility interview declaration.

After applying, your application is then assigned a priority code based on the information provided. Then, they are placed on NYCHA's preliminary waiting list for an interview to test for eligibility. After which you will receive an acknowledgment letter within two weeks. The application will be valid for two years from the day of receipt.

Public housing is a crucial resource for working families, elderly, disabled and a host of others whom the market does not, and will not attend to. It also protects economic diversities in several places especially inexpensive, fast-gentrifying cities like New York, San Francisco, and Washington.

CONCLUSION

It's a very difficult task to start over, especially when it has to do with a large loss. To start over is easier said than done, but only two options face you after a loss; pick up the pieces and realize you are privileged to start over again or throw yourself a pity party and stay in the bed of regret. When life throws you into such a situation, rather than panicking and looking at it as a punishment, thereby allowing fear to paralyze you, you had better see it as a new chance—as a new opportunity to showcase yourself in a new dimension, to craft your life on a stronger and healthier foundation. A new chance to be happy, to show the world that you are not shaken.

Starting over isn't easy, and it requires a lot of inner strength, courage, self-love, resilience, faith, and confidence. And since most of these things take time to develop, you will need to be patient and gentle with yourself. Treat yourself with love, compassion, and understanding.

If you look around, you will observe other people overcoming the adversities they are faced with, some of which are worse than yours. At the same time, you will see people that gave in to their adversities and turned to alcohols and drugs.

You will always be faced with problems. Now, what differentiates people is the responses to the problems. Do we let them crumple us under them, or do we step over them? Generally, the goal is to trade smaller problems for bigger and better problems. We are to man up to whatever challenge we are faced with. We are to grow up into one who can overcome whatever challenges come our way. We are to look around and say, "people have been dealing with hardship since the beginning of time, I don't know how to deal with this, but I imagine people exist that do." Your job then is to grow yourself as a person and be better prepared to overcome your problems. See it as a bumpy road, where all you need do is put one foot in front of the other, maintaining your goals in mind, learning along the way. So, no matter how well people appear, no matter how your situation might be different from that of your neighbor, understand that we all struggle, what we do with our struggles is what makes the difference.

Sometimes, it takes a "why me" moment for us to learn that there is a power that hides behind thinking we've lost it all. We must realize that each time we fall, no matter the greatness of the fall, the damages, it is expedient for us to rise, and there is a part of us ready to take this charge of rising. There is a part of us, that is always ready to fight challenges and overcome them. So, rather than wailing or being caught in the web of self-pity and regrets, activate that part of you, take the necessary time to heal from your loss, sit up and get your life back. Start by plotting, planning and setting out to start over with a fierce determination. The pity party event isn't good for you, so do away with it immediately. How? By training yourself to see the good in every situation. Mindset is everything about life. Try to see things from a positive dimension. View it as God handing you on a silver platter, a chance to go out, start over, experience more, learn more, feel more, and do more. You may have lost nearly all, but you've got a life, so empower your mindset and get going. Take the time, and reboot and reset your attitude. Losing it is very bad and devastating but lingering in the loss is harder and worse. When things are tough, it's sure easy to forget how important it is to stay positive, and not give up, but consider yourself reminded now. Unlike many, don't be a quitter. You might see a lot of people failing around you, even in the same circumstances but heck, that's why you are reading this now, and they aren't.

Giving up is truly the easy way out, but does it truly lead out? No! It drowns one in the pool of the failure or loss. Truly, a fresh start might be full of uncertainties, and this might not sit well with you but don't give up, it's the way out. It's the way up. It would sure be easier to say, "screw it, I can't keep fighting to recover the things I've lost and get myself back on track." You can even think about this every single day but don't ever let yourself heed to that because nothing good ever comes easy. And if you are given the opportunity to start afresh, find joy in something new, and set out on a new adventure. Common, why on earth would you give that all up because your house got burned?

Dispose of all fears, excuses, limitations, and plunge yourself boldly into the thick of life. Live each day as a new opportunity from God. Make the very best of every moment, of every experience and of every interaction that God sends your way. Take chances, don't be rigid, make mistakes. Have no fear. Live without regrets.

Let go of all mindsets and beliefs, excuses, ideas, and expectations that limit you and just relax into life. Be soft and flexible. Swim with the flow of life, and not against it. Fill your heart with love, gratitude, and appreciation, and constantly express them honestly and sincerely, all that life has given you, and will still give you. Worry less and be grateful for everything.

No matter how hard and difficult, embrace your present reality. Make peace with the present moment, and you will find peace throughout your journey. Always engage in vulnerable, humble, honest and meaningful conversations with the Source of all things - God. Let Him guide you, help you and assist you. And always be thankful for the wonderful and precious gifts life will continue to send your way.